D1443809

Searchlight BOOKS™

What Can
We Do about
Pollution?

How Can We Reduce

Household Waste?

Mary K. Pratt

Lerner Publications ◆ Minneapolis

Content Consultant: Roopali Phadke, Associate Professor of Environmental Studies, Macalester College

Lerner Publications Company
A division of Lerner Publishing Group, Inc.
241 First Avenue North
Minneapolis, MN 55401 USA

For reading levels and more information, look up this title at
www.lernerbooks.com.

Library of Congress Cataloging-in-Publication Data

Pratt, Mary K., author.
  How can we reduce household waste? / by Mary K. Pratt.
    pages cm. — (Searchlight books. What can we do about pollution?)
  Audience: Ages 8-11.
  Audience: Grades 4 to 6.
  Includes bibliographical references and index.
  ISBN 978-1-4677-9517-3 (lb : alk. paper) — ISBN 978-1-4677-9701-6 (pb : alk. paper) — ISBN 978-1-4677-9702-3 (eb pdf)
  1. Refuse and refuse disposal—Juvenile literature. 2. Recycling (Waste, etc.) —Juvenile literature. 3. Pollution prevention—Juvenile literature. I. Title.
  TD792.P73 2016
  363.72'88—dc23

                                    2015016197

Manufactured in the United States of America
1 – VP – 12/31/15

Contents

Chapter 1

HOUSEHOLD WASTE

Household waste includes all the trash created by the things we throw away. And we throw away many things. In the United States, the average person throws away about 4.5 pounds (2 kilograms) of stuff every day. Only 1.5 pounds (0.7 kg) of that gets recycled or composted. The remaining 3 pounds (1.4 kg) is household waste.

An average American throws away more than 1,000 pounds (450 kg) of household waste each year. How much household waste does the entire country create?

What happens when you add up all the household waste Americans create? It comes out to about 164 million tons (149 metric tons) each year. But this is only an estimate from the US government. No one knows the exact amount of household waste Americans create. In fact, some experts believe it might be up to seven times that amount! In any case, a huge number of unwanted items end up in the garbage. And all of this garbage has serious effects on our environment.

AMERICAN WASTE
(INCLUDING RECYCLABLES)

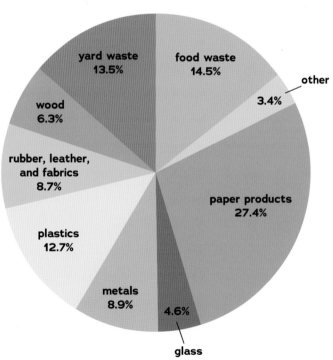

yard waste 13.5%

food waste 14.5%

other 3.4%

wood 6.3%

rubber, leather, and fabrics 8.7%

paper products 27.4%

plastics 12.7%

metals 8.9%

4.6%

glass

Types of Household Waste

There are four basic categories of household waste. The first category is paper, plastic, metal, and glass. The second category is food waste and yard waste. Cleaning products make up the third category. The fourth category is e-waste, or electronic waste. This includes items such as old cell phones and TVs.

Plastic bottles decompose slowly in landfills. They should be recycled.

A WORKER MOVES SHREDDED PAPER AT A RECYCLING CENTER. NEXT, WATER WILL BE ADDED TO THE PAPER, AND IT WILL BE TURNED INTO PULP.

Each of these types of waste has different effects on our planet. The good news is that we can fight the effects of every type of household waste. When we recycle and reuse waste, we keep these materials out of landfills. This helps clean the land, air, and water. It also improves our health. Let's explore each type of waste and find out what we can do to reduce its effects.

Chapter 2

PAPER, PLASTIC, METAL, AND GLASS

Paper makes up more than one-quarter of the materials Americans throw away. Paper trash includes things such as notebooks and magazines. It also includes the cardboard and paper packages on the things we buy.

Newspapers are one type of paper trash. What are some others?

Another quarter of waste comes from plastic, metal, and glass. This includes items such as plastic bags and old toys. It also includes glass jars and metal cans. Soda cans are usually made of a metal called aluminum. Foods such as beans and soup usually come in cans made of steel.

Americans recycle 71 percent of their steel cans. But they recycle only 50 percent of their aluminum cans.

Effects of Pollution from Paper, Plastic, Metal, and Glass

When products are thrown away, they often end up in landfills. These are places where trash is buried in the ground. Other trash items are burned in incinerators.

Landfills and incinerators cause problems for our planet. For instance, when paper rots in landfills or burns in incinerators, it sends out greenhouse gases. These gases trap heat in Earth's atmosphere. Greenhouse gases are important because they make our planet warm enough for life. But too much greenhouse gas leads to higher temperatures. Over time, these higher temperatures result in climate change.

A crane carries trash to an incinerator.

In the United States, more than half of all waste ends up in landfills.

Things made of plastic take a long time to decompose, or break down into smaller bits. So these products stay as they are for hundreds of years and take up space in landfills. They often leach, or leak, dangerous chemicals into the environment. When plastic is burned in incinerators, it releases chemicals into the air. Many of these chemicals are harmful to people and plants.

Sometimes trash does not even make it into landfills or incinerators. Many household items end up as litter in parks, forests, rivers, lakes, and oceans. The litter problem is so big that vast sections of the ocean are covered with bits of plastic.

This water sample from the Pacific Ocean contains hundreds of pieces of plastic.

When a bird eats trash, sharp pieces of plastic may cut the bird's throat.

All that litter puts toxic chemicals into the land, water, and air. This can make plants and animals, including humans, very sick. Animals can also get trapped in plastic trash and starve. Sometimes animals eat small pieces of trash because they think it is food. These animals often get sick and die as a result.

What Can We Do?

You can reduce the amount of trash you create. Start by buying only what you need. When you do buy something, look for items made from recycled materials. Also, look for products that have little or no packaging. One good choice is buying whole fruits and vegetables instead of those in boxes or bags. When shopping, bring reusable bags instead of using disposable plastic bags.

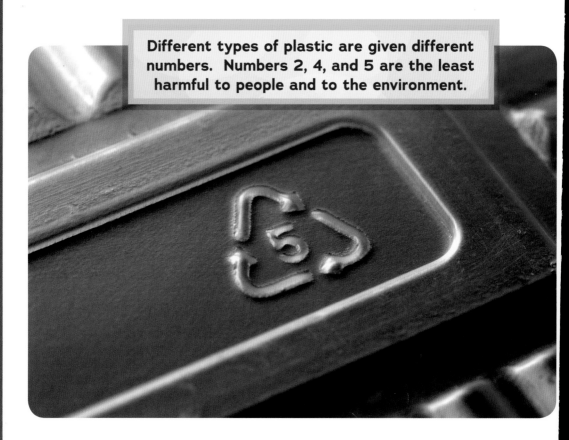

Different types of plastic are given different numbers. Numbers 2, 4, and 5 are the least harmful to people and to the environment.

When you are ready to get rid of something, look for ways to reuse it. For example, an old shoe box can become a storage bin. If you do not want an item that is in good condition, give it to someone else. If no one wants it, try to recycle it. If you have to throw it out, dispose of it properly so it does not become litter.

One way to reuse an old can is to make it into a flowerpot.

Recycled bottles can be made into many things, including patio furniture.

People are also finding ways to make better use of all our trash. For example, some clothing is made from recycled plastic bottles. Scientists are also studying whether a certain fungus can eat a common type of plastic. That would help cut back on all the plastic trash that fills up landfills.

Chapter 3

FOOD WASTE AND YARD WASTE

Food and plant materials make up another quarter of the trash in the United States. Food waste is all the food people throw out. It includes meal scraps and food that went bad before it could be eaten. Plant waste usually comes from the yard. It includes grass clippings, leaves, and branches.

Leaves are a common type of yard waste. What are some examples of food waste?

Effects of Food Waste and Yard Waste Pollution

In the United States, farmers produce more than 590 billion pounds (268 billion kg) of food every year. But Americans waste between one-quarter and one-half of that food. Farmers sometimes let fruits and vegetables rot in fields. They often do this when the food is not an ideal shape or color, because this makes it harder to sell.

These tomatoes have skin cracks, so the farmer left them in the field.

GROCERY STORES OFTEN THROW AWAY
FOODS THAT ARE CLOSE TO GOING BAD,
EVEN IF THEY ARE STILL GOOD.

Stores throw away lots of food too. They want customers to have plenty of choices. So, they stock more food than they plan to sell. They also get rid of many foods that do not look perfect.

The average American family throws away more than $1,300 worth of food every year.

People waste a lot of food at home as well. Families often fail to use their food before it goes bad. And many people buy more food than they can use.

When food and yard waste ends up in landfills, it rots. This creates methane, a powerful greenhouse gas. Methane contributes to climate change.

Solutions to Food Waste and Yard Waste Pollution

How can you help? Take only the food that you plan to eat. And try not to be too picky. For instance, cut a bruise out of an apple and eat the rest instead of throwing away the whole apple.

Governments are getting involved too. The city of Seattle, Washington, passed a law in 2015. It requires people to recycle food waste. The city fines people who do not follow the law.

A woman in Seattle shows her three waste bins. Waste in the two large bins will be recycled. Waste in the small black bin will end up in a landfill.

People can generate less yard waste by keeping leaves and grass clippings on the lawn. These materials provide natural nutrition to the landscape. People can shred leaves and grass clippings to make mulch. Mulch is a layer of material that is spread over the ground. It keeps the soil healthier.

A PERSON SPREADS MULCH OVER A GARDEN. MULCH CAN BE MADE FROM MANY THINGS, INCLUDING WOOD CHIPS, GRASS CLIPPINGS, AND HAY.

Composting usually takes two to six months.

You can also turn food and yard waste into dirt. This process is called composting. Some people use special bins for their food scraps and yard waste. Other people simply make a pile out in the open. Over time, these materials will naturally decay and turn into dirt. Then you can use the dirt to plant a garden!

Chapter 4

CLEANING PRODUCTS

Most people want to be clean and have a clean home. But the items we use to stay clean are not always good for the environment. Some of the chemicals in cleaning products can make people and animals sick.

Cleaning products often contain many chemicals. What problems can these chemicals cause?

Soaps and shampoos are not dangerous when you are cleaning yourself. But what happens after you use these products? Liquids get rinsed down the drain. Over time, the chemicals in these products build up in the environment.

Antibacterial soap has chemicals that cause damage to plants and animals. Regular soap is just as effective.

Effects of Pollution from Cleaning Products

Water treatment plants clean up much of the water that goes down the drain. But some chemicals remain. These chemicals can hurt fish and other animals that live in the water.

Some cleaning products spray chemicals into the air. People who use these chemicals may develop asthma. This condition makes it difficult to breathe. Cleaning chemicals build up in the atmosphere too. Over time, this can also cause health problems for people.

Water treatment plants have separate holding tanks for different steps of the cleaning process.

Solutions to Pollution from Cleaning Products

What can you do? Choose cleaning products that have few harmful chemicals. Look for certain words on product labels. Those words include *biodegradable* and *low toxicity.*

CLEANING PRODUCTS WITHOUT HARMFUL CHEMICALS STILL DO A GOOD JOB.

Making your cleaning products at home is better for the environment. It also saves money!

Also, look for products that list all their ingredients on their labels. That way, you will know exactly what is in the cleaner. Then you can research the ingredients online to make sure they are safe. You can even make your own natural cleaners for countertops, bathtubs, and toilets. Ask an adult to help you clean with nontoxic ingredients such as vinegar and baking soda.

Chapter 5

E-WASTE

People today have more electronic devices than ever before. Many homes have TVs, video game systems, and cell phones. These devices make up a growing part of our trash. And just like other kinds of trash, these devices can cause a lot of harm when they are thrown out.

Old cell phones are one example of electronic waste. What are some other examples?

Effects of E-Waste Pollution

Electronic waste, or e-waste, contains many toxic materials. But less than 15 percent of e-waste is recycled. That means most e-waste ends up in landfills or incinerators. When e-waste is buried or burned, the toxic materials can be released into the land, water, and air.

Old computer monitors contain small amounts of mercury. This metal is very harmful to people and animals.

When e-waste is incinerated, the fumes may contain cancer-causing particles.

E-waste contains a high amount of lead. If e-waste is not disposed of properly, lead can leach into people's water supplies. When people drink this water, it can damage their kidneys. It also damages their blood and their nervous systems.

A family in China sorts e-waste. Workers often handle dangerous materials without protective gloves or masks.

Unfortunately, recycling electronics can be harmful too. Some recycling programs in the United States send e-waste to other countries. Workers in those countries take apart the electronics in dangerous conditions. This process releases the toxic materials straight into the environment.

Solutions to E-Waste Pollution

You can reduce harmful e-waste. First, do not get rid of electronics that still work. Second, when you do get rid of electronics, look for recycling programs at local stores and government offices. These programs should guarantee that the e-waste will be handled responsibly. If your favorite electronics company does not have a recycling program, ask the company to start one.

TAKE GOOD CARE OF YOUR CELL PHONE SO IT WILL LAST A LONG TIME.

Chapter 6

REDUCE, REUSE, RECYCLE

You can help stop household waste pollution by following the three Rs: reduce, reuse, and recycle. These Rs are listed in order of importance. That means the most important step is reduce. The less we buy, the less trash we produce.

Recycling is one of the three Rs. Which of the three Rs is most important?

Do you have old toys that you do not use? Consider giving them to younger kids instead of throwing them away.

So the next time you are at the store, think about what you really need. If you can live without something, consider leaving it on the shelf.

The second most important step is reuse. When you do buy something, try to use it until it wears out. And if you do not need it anymore, give it to someone who will use it. That way, it will not go to a landfill.

A worker operates a machine at a recycling center.

The third most important step is recycle. When it is time to get rid of something, make every effort to recycle it rather than throwing it in the trash. In most areas, waste disposal companies provide separate recycling bins so people can easily recycle paper, glass, and some kinds of plastic and metal. Some items, such as paint and batteries, are harder to recycle. But many areas have centers where these items can be brought for recycling.

Working Together to Find Solutions

Many places have laws that require people to recycle. The city of Austin, Texas, has set a goal to cut the amount of trash it sends to landfills to nearly zero by the year 2040. The country of Sweden has nearly achieved this goal. It sends only 1 percent of its trash to landfills.

Household waste is a major problem. But we have the power to solve it. And the solution begins with making smart choices in our everyday lives.

AMERICAN RECYCLING RATES FROM 1960 TO 2010

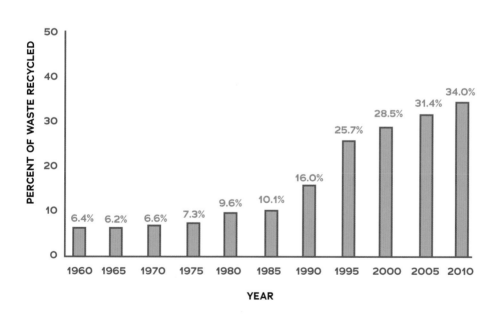

Glossary

compost: to turn food and yard waste into dirt by letting it decay

decay: to rot

decompose: to naturally break down into smaller parts

dispose: to put in a final place

incinerator: a facility that burns trash, often to produce electric power

landfill: a place where trash is stored in the ground

leach: to pass out or through

responsibly: in a manner that is right and trustworthy

toxic: harsh or harmful

Learn More about Household Waste

Books

Close, Edward. *What Do We Do with Trash?* New York: PowerKids Press, 2013. This book explores what happens to trash and how we can recycle.

Flounders, Anne. *Reducing Waste*. Minneapolis: Lerner, 2014. Interesting facts and colorful photos make this book an excellent way to learn about reducing waste.

Mulder, Michelle. *Trash Talk!: Moving Toward a Zero-Waste World*. Custer, WA: Orca Book Publishers, 2015. Mulder offers lots of creative ideas for dealing with trash.

Websites

How Kids Can Help Solve the E-Waste Problem
http://www.electronicstakeback.com/how-to-recycle-electronics/resources-for-kids/
This website explains several things you can do with old electronics when you are done using them.

Reduce, Reuse, Recycle
http://kids.niehs.nih.gov/explore/reduce/
Explore various ways to protect the environment by getting rid of household waste responsibly.

Reducing Waste: What You Can Do
http://www2.epa.gov/recycle/reducing-waste-what-you-can-do
Learn about all the ways you can help make a difference, including at home, at school, and in the community.

Index

Photo Acknowledgments

The images in this book are used with the permission of: © Dragon Images/Shutterstock Images, p. 4; © Red Line Editorial, pp. 5, 37; © auremar/Shutterstock Images, p. 6; © Photodisc/Thinkstock, p. 7; © Mitrija/Shutterstock Images, p. 8; © Piotr Malczyk/iStockphoto, p. 9; © Matthias Graben/Imagebroker/Corbis, p. 10; © millraw/iStockphoto, p. 11; © Jonathan Alcorn/Bloomberg/Getty Images, p. 12; © David W. Leindecker/Shutterstock Images, p. 13; © John Kwan/Shutterstock Images, p. 14; © asife/Shutterstock Images, p. 15; © Olivier Le Queinec/Shutterstock Images, p. 16; © hydrangea100/iStockphoto, p. 17; © akiyoko/Shutterstock Images, p. 18; © alexis84/iStockphoto/Thinkstock, p. 19; © CBCK-Christine/iStockphoto/Thinkstock, p. 20; © Ted S. Warren/AP Images, p. 21; © Katarzyna Bialasiewicz/iStockphoto/Thinkstock, p. 22; © Piotr Malczyk/iStockphoto/Thinkstock, p. 23; © Maxx-Studio/Shutterstock Images, p. 24; © Jonas Unruh/iStockphoto, p. 25; © antikainen/iStockphoto, p. 26; © Kraig Scarbinsky/Digital Vision/Thinkstock, p. 27; © Geo-grafika/iStockphoto, p. 28; © ermingut/iStockphoto, p. 29; © akiyoko/iStockphoto, p. 30; © BanksPhotos/iStockphoto, p. 31; © Chien-min Chung/In Pictures/Corbis, p. 32; © LattaPictures/iStockphoto, p. 33; © FangXiaNuo/iStockphoto, p. 34; © romrodinka/iStockphoto, p. 35; © Brasil2/iStockphoto, p. 36.

Front Cover: © Walter Zerla/Blend Images/Getty Images

Main body text set in Adrianna Regular 14/20.
Typeface provided by Chank.